COLLECTION OF SUFI POEMS

Arriving At The Throne Of Love

H.B. Johar

Awardee Of The
South East Asia Write Award 2010

Edited by
Fazidah Abu Bakar

Translated by
Fazidah Abu Bakar with Nur Aisha Rahmat

Lulu

Collection Of Sufi Poems
Arriving At The Throne Of Love
by H.B. Johar
Copyright ©2011 H.B. Johar

Paperback: ISBN 978-981-07-0103-1

Edited by
Fazidah Abu Bakar
Translated by
Fazidah Abu Bakar with Nur Aisha Rahmat

Self Published by H.B. Johar | Johar Buang©2011
Email: hbjohar@hotmail.com | Singapore
@Book Publishing - Lulu.com | USA
Website: http://www.lulu.com

Translated from the original of a collection of poems
"Sampai Di Singgahsana Cinta"
by Johar Buang @H.B. Johar ©2011
Award-winning of The Singapore Literature Prize 2010
Publisher Pustaka Islamiyah Sdn Bhd | Malaysia
© PI 2009 | Malay Edition
ISBN 978-983-9068-12-2
Email: pustakaislamiyah@me.com

Cover photo taken by H.B. Johar
"Chao Phraya River"
2010 S.E.A. Write Award
5th November 2010
@Mandarin Oriental, Bangkok
Thailand

Arriving At The Throne
Of Love

Ya Wadud

O The Loving
The One who desires good for all mankind

For my wife

Hajah Fazidah Abu Bakar

Love is His Love too

~H.B. Johar

Contents

Preface

Arriving At The Throne Of Love

H.B. Johar also known by his name Johar Buang, is increasingly regarded as a Sufi poet in the region. This is a significant and meaningful development in his literary journey spanning more than three decades.

His latest anthology, *Arriving At The Throne Of Love*, which you are reading now, promises a different approach in his efforts to delve into the depth of the human heart with regard to relationships with people, nature and most importantly, the Creator.

Sufi tradition in the arts has indeed made a big contribution to Islamic civilization and the universe. Even today, poems by the great Sufis such as Jalaludin Rumi, Ahmad Jami and Umar Khayyam are still being read throughout the world. Works of Rumi have been reprinted dozens of times in the West and are often used in meditation sessions by motivational therapy practitioners such as Dr. Deepak Chopra.

In this region, among the Sufi poets who is still well remembered is Hamzah Fansuri, a renowned man of piety from Barus, Aceh, in the 16th century AD, who was also a traveller to the Middle East and Malay Archipelago. Although the works of Hamzah were burnt during the fall of the sultanate of Aceh, his legacy is still felt today. Obviously, this proves that his outstanding mystic work has its own charm in terms of aptness of his choice of words which reflects profound sincerity.

The process of producing Sufistic poetry is not as easy as portrayed by some people - just write beautiful words and relate them to aspects of divinity and the soul. Sufi poets should first equip themselves with two main prerequisites. First, he must go through the experience of mysticism. In this case, it can be said that Johar has gone through varied mystic experiences under the guidance of well-known Mursyid or mystic teachers. Such experiences require extensive reading of Sufi discipline which actually covers many areas - from knowing oneself to Sufi healing.

A strong student-mystic teacher relationship can help to produce an amazing and impactful experience for the student. However, not all students can produce Sufi poetry. This is where the student's talents and perseverance to learn language and literature play a vital role in spurring him or her to enter the literary world of mysticism.

Johar related only a bit of his unique experience in receiving 'guidance' from his teachers. Typically, practitioners of the religious order are very humble and secretive about their religious experience, let alone for public knowledge. This is in line with the religious discipline that places a high regard for immaculate manners, including humility.

Even in his poetry, Hamzah Fansuri merely mentioned that the search in his long journey was for the purpose of seeking the Grace of His Lord. Finally, he found God in his heart (at home). This was evident in the Holy Quran which states that an individual who has bound his soul with Allah will feel that all his actions are motivated by Allah (Surah Al-Fath 48:10). This sincere person has attained knowledge of himself and his Creator to a point where he views the needs of this world as full of temporariness and he yearns for a beautiful life in the hereafter.

In fact, the person whose heart worships Allah alone until the end, will be rewarded with heaven, (Surah Al-Syuraa 26:88-89). Isn't this the dream of every Muslim, what more those who practise Sufism? However, this does not mean that a Muslim should neglect his responsibilities to his family and community. It is in this world that everyone is granted the chance to prove himself as a devout man (a faithful and righteous servant). This process is indeed difficult because of the numerous tribulations that everyone has to endure. Human tribulations become more varied with the changing of times. In ancient times such as that of Hamzah Fansuri, life's tribulations came in the form of an ascribed system bound by feudalism and so on, yet a mystic was still able to 'conceal' himself. Now with the exponential growth of population, it is difficult for anyone to find a remote place to lead a solitary existence like a hermit. In fact modern man is increasingly confronted with environmental problems such as greenhouse gas pollution to the threat of nuclear weapons. Such problems were revealed in the poems by Johar who tried to find 'peace' in the teachings of Sufism in order to face the hustle and bustle of life.

As a complete lifestyle that is blessed by Allah, Islam offers options for people to get through life in a modest and meaningful way. Johar tried to present this in his poems that the human sojourn on earth in the form of a long journey, still holds hope. Thus, what is required are the stock of knowledge, faith and good deeds.

The turmoil faced by Muslims in the early part of the 21st century (there is one Muslim for every four persons in the world, according to Pew Research Center Survey, United States) is appalling. Muslims are increasingly being portrayed as radicals and disrespectful of the religious rights of others. Such a statement does not hold true. Historical records did not cite Muslims as the cause of both World Wars. In fact, much suffering in the world was inflicted on the Muslims by the impact of Western colonialism.

We also cannot deny the fact that some of the problems plaguing the Muslim community were the results of errors made by the leaders and the Muslims themselves. Problems of unfairness or injustice occurred in many countries where majority of the people are Muslims. Not a single Muslim-majority country has reached the level of progress on par with the Western developed countries in giving priority to universal education, housing, healthcare and women's rights. Thus, the dream that the Muslims would return to build great civilizations such as those in the 7th century until the 14th century, still raises a question mark.

Johar's poems proved that mistakes made by the Muslims and not their religion, were the contributing factors to this present state of confusion. Despite the appeal that was made according to the Sufi tradition, Johar tried to present the meaning of 'rejuvenation' or reform that is very important in building a meaningful life. It is hoped that this anthology will benefit you in your efforts to achieve a successful life, God willing. Amen. Congratulations to the author for his perseverance.

Mohd Raman Daud
Feature Editor, Berita Harian Singapore

Poetry Is My Personal Praises To God

Poetry is my personal way of glorifying God who created this entire universe, apart from performing other religious obligations, invoking Him day and night as well as expressing salutations to His esteemed beloved one, Prophet Muhammad, peace be upon him, a blessing to the entire universe, light upon light, without his light it is impossible that I was born on this earth.

Poetry is a realm of invocation that is so widely spread. More extensive than the size of the Sahara Desert. Through poetry, I can chat with God when my heart feels lonely, happy or sad. Poetry brings me closer to the meaning of life. In poetry, I can wander to wherever The Lover wishes to bring my soul within His universe.

I have tried to write in other genres apart from poetry. Yet I did not enjoy the same kind of beauty, happiness, serenity, sweetness, sense of wonder and most importantly, devotion when I am near Him, like the way I feel in the realm of poetry. My prostration of appreciation to God who is willing to lend me whatever that belongs to Him in order for me to continue writing. Thus, I am not able to depart from poetry as it is the most precious thing in my life. Poetry is the central harbour of life, the destination for the vessels of thought and human emotions.

Together with this personal collection of poems *'Arriving At The Throne Of Love',* I hope it can transform into gardens of roses. If you are willing to touch it or smell its fragrance for a while, then pluck it and pin it onto the horizon of your heart. Otherwise, do view it from the depth of your knowledge.

H.B. Johar
15 October 2009

Convey My Greetings

convey the greetings of the verses of my poems
which sing about the sun
which have an eternal light

convey the greetings of the verses of my poems
to the earth
that He is the glorious saviour
love that is hurt

convey the greetings of the verses of my poems
whose path lead to the interior of the forest
that He is the hidden secret
hidden
to the entire image of this life

convey the greetings of the verses of my poems
because of His Love I am still here
enduring in the continent of poetry

Cheng Ho 1

is your sea voyage more appealing than viewing
the boundary of divine knowledge?
You have interpreted the hieroglyphs of the ocean
which glorified the story of a sailor, not in your world
a hot climate and the aridity of sand dust.

you too have
not sent the water here, while I am
Sahara who spreads love.

Cheng Ho 2

truly your kingdom
is just a handful of soil, don't you let
the earth suffer humiliation by the enraged
love of Tsunami
and the gardens of paradise are not gleaming
beneath the dawn of truth

Roots

under that dim city light an old male vendor
hugged his body shivering in the rain. he was awakened
by the thunder in the sky, trees swayed, the leafy
branches snapped, the birds were fearful. he was anxious
by the storm and fog, by the tramping sound of thousands
of shoes walking on the black asphalt road, he appeared
to be flinging something into a distant future and
reminiscing the unknown.

in the middle of the hustle and bustle of this city
everything is criss-crossing, like vehicles that are drunk
and restless, trapped in the stuffy lanes, no waxing moon
at the horizon concrete slabs of those buildings, hanging
only the grief and woes of the evening, only the fog
turning the clock of life and this falling rain
punished the conduct of the natives like the one who ate
the forbidden fruit fallen from the ancient garden,
charmed by the sweetness, finally defaming the body,
howling at the remains of the sacrifice!

he then packed the bundle, only keeping
the roots that now have no value, looking dull and
obsolete. the roots were displayed at the five foot way
to be sold to the city dwellers as panacea or
to discover oneself who was separated from the universe,
for the arrow was broken by the ogre, for the barking-
deer was unable to be hunted anymore.

the roots have lost their world and today
when it rained in the evening, he picked the bundle
and groped his way home.

Aquarium

while arranging the potted plants at the balcony, we have
yet to hear the clamour of the rocks colliding each
morning. How is nature's true feelings towards us? Ah, we
just remain calm here while sticking up the leafy roots,
transferring the soil in the pots, cutting wilted flowers
and dried leaves, our thoughts too should get out of the
window grilles that are facing the busy highway, don't
know why at this moment I wish to be a kite on the wings
of Gabriel, when earth has just appeared as an atom
where were we? How many millions of years does light
travel through the cosmos to reach the niche of the heart?
Just because of eating wrongly we once slipped from the
sky, our minds are more stark naked than the body, it is
best that we turn into fishes that escaped from the arrest
of time, assembled at the parliamentary conference for
the sake of planning for peace and not war, up to this day
exploding bombs can still be heard on the surface of the
earth, butterflies fluttering out from the cocoons
searching for the past direction of the tropics.

now we could hardly breathe in the rocky aquarium,
chairs in the office are silent and isolated, do you know in
the past there was a great debate in the hall of angels,
what exactly was recorded in the working paper of God's
agenda? Man are too greedy in monopolising the legal
resources, human rights are turned into political free
goods, in this marine nation there is no more coastal land
to disembark, we just measure fate in between the scales
of the fishes, who is going to change the fate of the coral
reefs, translating thousands of academic books from the
mildew of historical phenomena? We are trapped in the
balcony of this apartment, unable to read the map on
forestry, unable to understand the direction of the wind,
how cruel time is to become the executioner, did you hear
the mourners wailing at the end of the river? There are
angry faces hiding in the worms' cramped forts. Who
terrorized the war planes that flew past the atmosphere,

bombing the flesh of the earth, toxic chemicals also peeled the earth's epidermis? On the roof of the divine sky souls went on a hunger strike and descended to the field on polling day, at night before sleeping we often wondered on a foul mattress, who is the nation's winning presidential candidate in the future, someone to whom the people can express their humanitarian plight? From the edge of the window grilles, a balcony remains silent. All this while are we pretending to befriend nature? We fantasized flower pots, pots with greenish foliage to create a harmonious dream garden, when in fact we have isolated it far from its original roots, our own lives are confined in a rocky aquarium, we are the fishes that could not cross the river, too faithful to the solid rock of civilization, but our blood will continue to flow to whichever gully, will come knocking on the glass door of parliament, looking at one anxious face of the world, what is the meaning of our existence? Sleeping babies in the womb were startled, snapped out like a battalion of worms which heard the sound of the trumpet, from the muddy clay we were raised to the top of the ivory tower, stately pillars are the symphonic theme for the country, but now where are the former homes and grassy meadows that bear us? Across that sea often it was heard there were quakes splitting the earth, cannonballs exploding in mosques, stirring a commotion in temples and churches, we killed our own brothers in the name of the war of the century that is meaningless!

earth cannot afford to survive for another one thousand years, let us plan a universal prayer, seeking a direction for the heart of the earth, before God feels bored and thus closes the door of the throne, before the singing of the frogs beckons snowfall in the desert of Sahara, before the mountains argue with the moon, the sun and the stars, let not the belly of the sky shake and shriek, spewing bubbles of faith.

Hieroglyphs Of A River

"That river is totally clear," said those
who read about it from the ancient scriptures.
The sky above that sky there exists a garden
stemmed a tree as upright as the hieroglyph Alif[1]
its lush foliage shines in the shade
not transparent like the violet peacock feathers
hiding its golden sheen.
Beneath it there flows afar seven levels of rivers
to all the rifts of the earth, its source only a drop of water,
fallen from the assembly of the Throne, whence He hides
in the Valley of the Mirror and wishes to make known His
Existence before the creation, so He then rolls the carpet
of worldly life, hence creating the last realm as the frontal
veil for His shadow.
How strange, each path that leads there,
at that Alif tree, the flow comes and goes
without the need to capture time. At the base of the water
lies a royal treasure of most hidden beauty,
all containing everlastingness. None is
seen different and all sight
is the same sight, all feelings
are the same feelings.

"Only those seven levels of rivers can
heal the times," said those who understand
the meaning of the hieroglyphs. We are part of the
swirling waves, flowing and meandering, like the
teardrops of Adam at the door of repentance after being
expelled from the mirth of paradise, like Jonah who was
swallowed into the darkness
of the whale's belly, we enter the universe which unites
with the oceans, release anything that chains
the door of the soul, the intellect makes us confused who
are we? Hence, stand witness with the soul which was
breathed into the pores of our skin, the true nature of this

---

[1] First alphabet Arabic script.

river is honey which You poured from the ocean of Your
Love. And like Moses
who wandered in the valleys of the mountains, make
apparent the cloak of Your personality leading these
times, for the sake of capturing the light of Your Face that
can be known in every inch
of life, You are truly the secret hieroglyph, while others
are just witnesses to Your existence in the garden of good
deeds.

Cosmetic

(a night with the poet Djamal Tukimin,
sitting and discussing literature, sipping tea and eating
hot prata[2] at a stall - in front of Kassim Mosque,
Kampung Kembangan)

it is true, brother, love is divine knowledge and
we are a flock of birds without any status
whatsoever, even if our country of origin
is just a mirror which is buried deep
within the innermost self, a hiding place
most extraordinary, even if
without realising when unveiling the self
the eye of our hearts is the one gazing
upon His Face.

hence brother, no matter how the face of a person
is adorned with various
veiled cosmetic colors before the mirror,
surely God too is seen
because His Face is in oneself
much closer than our own jugular veins.

it is also not easy, o brother, to unravel
the moon to the specks of dust without the cosmetic
colours

so that even yonder, there is someone refracted by the
light
that opens the self.

---

[2] Indian bread

Dust

when You exhale Your breath
Your existence appears most clear
like the wind manifesting the dust

dust gathers
the earth, sun, moon and the stars
to become the platform of Love
meeting in the circumambulation of Love

in the scattered dusts of Love
there are some which You pull back
up into the Sky

Love Of A Pair Of Shoes 1

that genuine path is in your shoes
where no one else can see it
while your shoes are warming up the dusts of love

along the journey you see
there is nothing at all in front
perhaps you just wish to look back
yet behind everything is all the same
you do not hear anything
except the voice of your shoes,

"We were married as a pair of shoes
throughout that journey of love
it is better
than a door which is closed."

Love Of A Pair Of Shoes 2

that shoe shop is a temporary nurturing home
now I am enslaved wherever I go
I rebel, pleading to be freed
from the mazy path of life
so dusty and confusing

I am a crazy pair of shoes in fetters
for so long I have been very quiet
now I know not what I am saying
my only wish is to change into a different pair of shoes
from the ordinary shoes in this world

slip me on Cinderella's foot
tonight I wish to meet Love
in the eyes of a prince

Dervish

I was engrossed writing poems when you entered the
office then you hang your robe next to the veiled window
that was blocked facing the sun. Instantly you asked,
"What is nothing but needs something?"
"Certainly it is love," I answered.
"But I am not a lover. I am just the bearer of that robe,"
was your quick reply then you hurriedly left my office,
for a moment you forgot to slip-on your robe again
which you had removed from your traveller's body and
now it is left alone in the confined air conditioned room.

"My name has been removed from the list of those in
poetic robes. I have been killed and my poems have
turned into a cemetery," that was what you said when you
came knocking again on my office door the following day.
I observed your serene face smiling, in your right hand
tightly clasped was a knife of experience.

"I should be smiling, even if You place a sword
on my neck. I will not take my eyes off from looking at
Your Face.

Leave me alone, this world does not exist. Thus all the
other realms truly do not exist. Let me go far, far away,
what I am looking for is only myself."

perhaps I have found the paper with your last poem
which you left in the pocket of your robe that does not
contain anything else,
hanging at the veiled window in my office forever
you went to the traveller's meadow that is warm.

Drama

when the moment of patience arrives
carrying the flags of victory at the final battlefield
after fighting till death defending Your truth
then at that moment all veils were drawn
there is no beauty that can match Your beauty
and not even a bit of ugliness can disguise
in the vision of Your Truth
You have made that enmity and hatred
only as a temporary drama
when Your lovers see Your Face

Dance Of Symphony

love is not a hall of debates
which is mutually difficult to accept opinions
love owns layers of images of its doors
each of its doors which is opened
have birds encircling
pulling you into the dance of a symphony...

Metaphor

it is true that I do not like to drink instant coffee
just pour it into another cup
I want to mix honey at the breakfast table
so that we will be free from all sickness and suspicions

at dawn on the radio a religious teacher taught
a Sufi's prayer most efficacious, Allah is enough
for me
I touched the jugular vein and felt Him much closer
than a strand of hair, a century not possible
for me to tread the poems of Ibnu Arabi
heading towards the red sulphur

why
is there a dark colour in the morning coffee that you sip
from that transparent cup
as coffee in a cup, there is a hole
that cannot be penetrated. This country is quiet, you said
let us kneel beneath the breeze
or go to the shores
catching the resounding invocation of the fishes
at the meeting of two oceans

What You See Are Merely Paper Birds

what you see are merely paper birds
flying across the domain of the sky - but who is
poetry, really?

as long as we spread the wings of words
flying everywhere, when will we arrive
at the nation of longing

thank you God
for making my heart
dust so fine
hardly penetrable
because in it
You manifest the Sahara

if split a dot in the heart's domain
a hundred rivers will overflow
fishes will be seen
in the clear water

This Nation Is Your Nation

this nation is without a king, royal power
and a throne
the king is the people, the people are the king

this nation is beneath the sun, moon and
twinkling stars
however its light has never
created shadows

this nation has no garden
no shores nor oceans

God, thank you
You made this nation Your nation
in the heart of a lover who owns nothing

The Personality

when time was yet to be created by You
only love was eternal
in the ocean of voices You encompassed the word
"Be!..."
in another nation You summarised various images
I am an atom which has broken the tears
floundering the moment the facial skin was peeled
a piece of flesh of the intellect suddenly opened the door
the immense universe called self, stepped down
from every stairway of the sky, treading the earthly roots
wandering with the manifested self
not because of the expulsion from the sky, not because of
mistakenly eating the forbidden fruit, not because
of the serpent's instigation beneath the shady tree in
paradise, not because of the arrogance of the devil
refusing to prostrate at your feet, Adam,
not also because of the intense love for Hawa till
the inner garment slipped down without
a single thread on the body

o Alif,
when I cut the flesh of this intellect of mine
'I am man thus naked!'
but not from the physical element of the universe
not destroyed even if it was sliced and diced
You breed hundreds of budding personalities

cloaked in light, I too slipped it on
so then I know Your Presence
in this worldly body after all, not outside

King Of The Heart

the heart which has been crowned as king
is the heart which reaches to meet Me
not enticed by offers
seven stations of the sky
no one is in them
except Me

Drum

those skilful hands only know how to strike,
derum deram derum deram
how that hide is like a fortress forever defending the
truth, for the voice roaring in a cell, for the love which has
grown wings, soaring forcefully
from the door of the earth.

that drum is just a hide, its secret lies right
in the centre, in reality the universe has no sound,
no letter, no voice
- disappointed, empty.

listen to the beating of the soul, before it touches Alif
there is a hole in the sky
"Where was I?"
before the universe was fully created.

The Niche

Allaaah[3]....the breath that is exhaled
Huuu[4]....the breath that is inhaled
enters into The Truth between the mind
which inside it is a gem
in that gem is the mind
in that mind is passion
in that passion are feelings
in those feelings is the heart
in that heart is light
in that light is a secret
in that secret is Me
which encompasses all there is
the Alif of my body that moves and is silent

are you the eagle
that came to put back in order
the throne of the kingdom
a moment sir, I am getting ready for the migration
to find a door out

who will not be the chosen one
watching the waxing moon emerging from the mirror
who is not surprised being mesmerized
by the melody of the flute

yet the piper is nowhere to be seen
who will not be ecstatic while being swept away
by the storm
fishes leaping out from the oceanic sky

bird in a cage or a cage in a bird
light in a glass or glass in light
grapes in a cup or cup in grapes
o Lord, which is Allah which is Me

---

[3] God
[4] He (God)

which is Muhammad which is Ahmad

The Master's Flute

the soft melody of the flute
mesmerising
yet its piper is nowhere to be seen

thousands of birds in flocks
spreading wings
flying out from the cage
breezing into the flute's holes
with the same intention and melody
at the peak of Attar[5] mountain

at the peak of Attar mountain
who becomes the bird
who becomes the cage
the truth is
in flight
the bird is the cage
the cage is the bird

---

[5] Persian Sufi Poet – Fariduddin Attar

Birds Of The Heart

birds of the heart fold their wings
when soaring up to Your Kingdom
Love is thus melted
when facing You

Haze

the moment You are present in the alley of my heart
I am the green prayer mat for You to tread
for so long I fell asleep waiting for You
as soon as I awake, You jolt all my dreams
actually there are still many tasks
I have yet to prepare
far from view, the mid-morning time is fast rising
beneath the wings of a bird

before You unveil my entire face
I must expel all evil elements
I am ashamed the moment You look at me
You may refuse to enter the innermost chamber
of my heart again
I must soon clean the mirror, open the windows
invite the fragrant air, remove all dust
which had thickened at every corner of the veil
I must persevere to be close to You

even if the weather gets warmer by the window
of my room
the birds are restless chirping aloud
their migratory songs
the arid land yearns for the rain to fall at once
at a place where farmers moan, at a place
where settlers burn canopies of the forest swamp,
flames with hazy smoke

blemish the earth, swallowing
a promise of love most pure
extend the blade of the sword
pull this robe of mine with might and main
I wish to join You battling the outside world
I wish to fight a thousand traitors
who plot to destroy
Your hidden treasures
in the heart of the hazy forest

where the stench of breath is putrid
deers leaped from frighteningly dark valleys
extending remnants of wounded flesh
the floor of Your paradise suddenly spew out lava and
shrieking bats
hovering over their own dead bodies
enemies steal the moon
from the treasures of Your kingdom
felling trees of invocations, dancing wildly
in the fiesta of the haze
fire engulfed another fire, brutal
in covetous desires

haze is everywhere, on the field of weeds
all lost their way
shackled by a barren land, charred grass
I tread once again the waterless river
only the river knows about
the secret of the spilled milk
from Your hidden treasures

Kris[6]

brother, you have killed Jebat[7], right?
but wait a moment. This scene has not ended
who will kill you then, brother
with that Taming Sari Kris[8]
as long as you, brother, duplify the existence of Allah Most
Exalted
by glorifying the king
who is arrogant with his desire to be god?

that kris is still stained with the blood of Jebat
when you, brother, left that palace duel
you allowed Jebat's blood to hail his native land
have you forgotten of Jebat whom you stabbed in the
stomach
Jebat is the image of your flesh so alike
because of a stunted charmed kris
you stabbed your own brother

it is true, brother, you have killed Jebat
but Jebat still runs amok
in this Malay land

"hey, Tuah![9]
I will not die from the thrust of your enchanted kris
my life is kept
in the Hidden Treasures
beneath the folds of my flesh Allah sits enthroned
the secret of my heart is His Palace
far without any boundary, so near yet untouchable
even if my blood drips exclaiming His Name
yet He has neither form nor colour

---

[6] is a traditional weapon of the Malay culture.
[7] refers to Hang Jebat is a Malay warrior of the Malacca Sultanate era was killed
at the hands of his friend Hang Tuah as a rebel against the sultan.
[8] Taming Sari Kris (translation: Flower Shield Kris) is one of the most well-
known kris in Malay literature.
[9] refers to Hang Tuah is a legendary warrior/hero who lived during the reign of
Sultan Mansur Shah of the Sultanate of Malacca in the 15th century.

His presence in me is like the puppeteer directing the
theatre performance
He does not live in the sky, nor on the earth
but here, in my body His name is Me
never have I leaked this secret knowledge
of my warriorship
ever since we studied at Gunung Ledang!"[10]

---

[10] Gunung Ledang or Mount Ophir is a mountain situated in the Gunung Ledang
National Park located in Ledang District (northwestern Johor), Malaysia.

Eye Of The Window

the eye which is unable to reach
to look upon You
is the eye that is lost from You
yet You are always looking
in the direction of that eye of the window

Malays Have Gone To The Moon
With Their Spaceship

Malay originates from mim and mim[11] is a nation of
divine knowledge
like Raniri[12] please do not keep searching out for our
faults
based on the religious teachings of your ancient scripture
it is not heresy for a Malay to go to the moon
Malays do not dream of kissing the face of the moon

since the time of the sultanate of Aceh
Hamzah Fansuri[13] has created the classic vessel
this is the Malay vessel even though it is small yet
undeterred
sailing through stormy waves on the Indian Ocean and
the Nile River
successfully bringing home Allah's trophy to the Malay
Archipelago
which sank to the sea floor of the Khulzum Ocean
as a result of the brutal military attack by Mongolia
destroying all the sacred treasures of Islam
in the land of Baghdad the focal point for Sufis worldwide

Hamzah is not an infidel
as you alleged
Hamzah is a non-bearer of heresy
as you claimed
with all due respect to His Majesty Sultan Iskandar Thani

---

[11] Arabic alphabet script.

[12] Nuruddin ibn Ali ar-Raniri (died 1658) was an Islamic scholar from Gujarat, India. Ar-Raniri was born into a Gujarati family of Hadhrami lineage. He arrived in Aceh in 1637 and enjoyed the patronage of Sultan Iskandar Thani (reigned 1636-1641). He denounced his predecessors at the Acehnese court, Hamzah Pansuri and Syamsuddin of Pasai, for what he saw as their heresy in violation of the Islamic belief and ordered their books to be burned. He left Aceh in 1644 and died in India in 1658.

[13] Hamzah Fansuri (1590) was a famous Malay Sufi poet/writer, the first known to pen mystical panentheistic ideas in the Malay Literature. He wrote both prose and poetry and worked at the court of the Aceh Sultanate.

Hamzah did not go astray by wearing the Sufi's robe
as you slandered
according to the law in your karma scripture
which is tainted with envy and jealousy
Malays can fly to the sky
not just to sojourn on the surface of the moon
in fact the arrival is to convey greetings
to Gabriel
knocking on the door of Sidratul Muntaha[14]
Malays are the people of the Messenger of God who came
from the eastern end
Malays are the people of the Messenger of God who are
most heroic and united
Malays are the people of the Messenger of God who are
most courageous and do not despair
Malays are the people of the Messenger of God who are
most righteous and devout
Malays are the people of the Messenger of God who truly
love knowledge and world peace
Malays are the people of the Messenger of God
who never betray the Messenger of God

even as Raniri you are able to instigate the sultan
to spill the blood of Hamzah and his students
in the beloved land of Aceh
yet you are powerless
in defeating us as a nation
this is our Trade Ballad[15]
this is our Boat Ballad[16]
this is our Yellow Bird Ballad[17]
became flesh and blood and the pride of our heritage

Malay originates from mim and mim is a nation that has
divine knowledge
today you can no longer deny

---

[14] Lote tree that marks the end of the seventh heaven.
[15] Trade Ballad | Syair Dagang by Hamzah Fansuri
[16] Boat Ballad | Syair Perahu by Hamzah Fansuri
[17] Yellow Bird Ballad | Syair Burung Pingai by Hamzah Fansuri

Malays have gone to the moon in their spaceship

At The End Of
Hamzah Fansuri's[18] Love

His Secret and that is the truth
expressing a deep sense of reverence to His Own Being
He is hidden in the hidden
He is the reality of man but is unknown
The True One as the place of return
for all the truth

---

[18] Malay Sufi Poet (1590 – 1636)

Teachings

not a worm that destroys the capsized boat
then appears Siti Jenar[19] who tries to pry
at the fence during the teachings of the assembly of saints
but ask the ripples of water in the middle of the marsh
what is happening?
the water is turning ancient
keeping the facial skin of the sun
knows the direction and means of breathing
water is the valley of The Most Merciful
which has never stopped flowing
thus if fate capsizes that boat
why the hurry to fix
the thick sludge on the wall that absorbs the water?
like the wall which was raised by Khidir[20]
that is the wall behind which is preserved
a hidden treasure so priceless

we are surrounded and effaced in the throne of water
so engrossed and awe-inspiring
impossible for us to resist
the overflowing Kautsar[21] and the surge of His grace

after meeting in the dot of each
layer of the jewel of the heart
it is undeniable the light of His secret stays silent
and unites
in the niche of the truth of the perfect man
even though bestowed with temporal existence
in the body
but still everlasting since time immemorial
and protected by The Most Beloved
to see Himself outside the self
there is no true life except only Him
most self-supporting and sustaining the kingdom

---

[19] a Sufi and one of the spreading of Islam in Java.
[20] a messenger of God.
[21] name of one of the rivers in paradise.

of this heart
without form and colour except taste
not separated from His existence
besides taste that is the secret which is visible
on the jewelled image
a personality so noble
a fusion is forged between a truly devoted prayer
and the soul which witnesses its Lord
in beauty most perfect

anywhere in this universe
revealed and vastly spread
without an obstructing veil it becomes
an aromatic prayer mat
which reflects the glorious love of the Divine Being
so each worshipper is a lover
who is attached to the Lord
heading to a niche of The One

like thirty wings of birds
landed before the Emperor
love becomes courageous
by the majestic door witnessing the truth
and not requiring the dais of throne

the true Emperor
is not outwardly apparent from self lineage
exploring the whole universe
with the fleet of intellect
towering till the peak of the ego-pyramid
diving into the earth till the base of its seven oceans
even meditating deep in the quiet swampy forest
as long as the self is not reflected
and far from the address of love
who will drive to His Abode,
a chamber that does not allow Jibril in
even a step, "You will not see Me
except for My beloved chosen one."

Well

set your sight into that well
who do you see
in the deep water

you say love is like Tsunami
if the ocean runs amok
the ship is tossed onto the shore
fishes are not breathing
swimming on the beach
limp bodies
is this transient in transient
to you this is love

in this nation
only the rim of the well
is unlettered and voiceless
no email nor internet
no tv cable
no telephone
no newspaper
no
directory book

spread the sail
onto the well
the vessel is looking for the master
on the western horizon

even though
anchored on the eastern bank

Dew Of Manifestation

if you come to Him
only to present your wishes
then you are truly veiled from Him
you are unable to see Him
even if the darts of your eyes
are as sharp as the sun
wiping out the dew of manifestation

gaze only upon His Face
that is your most genuine prayer
meeting without a veil

in the niche of Masjidil Haram[22]
some pray in front of the Kaabah[23]
some pray in the Kaabah
some pray without seeing the Kaabah at all

the lover brings his prayer mat everywhere
walking in the quiet alley of his heart
you will gaze upon His niche
while you stand on a prayer mat
who is worshipping
and who then is being worshipped

when the eyes of your existence are closed
the eye of your heart then opens
and you can see Him
like how He will manifest Himself
to the dwellers of paradise
be a dweller of His Abode
and leave the shadows of the creations
on the plain of personal egoism
when He lifts His veil
hence all the sacred days

---

[22] Grand Mosque in Mecca.
[23] cube-shaped building in Mecca and is the most sacred site in Islam.

are divine knowledge
our duty is to open the door of this self
because His kingdom is inside

said the ant to Solomon
"We are tiny creatures
almost invisible to the world
so how is it possible that His majestic love
can reside in our existence?"

O my Lord
truly in prayer
I should heed to Your every wish
not You who must fulfill
all my desires
on the plains of doubt
the robes assembled lamenting
the time has come
yet You have not yet fulfilled the promise
the eye of the heart then melts and is blurred
voices ask

"Why are You silent and delaying
till it makes us so angry
perhaps because our deeds are insufficient
or were we negligent in perfecting our obligations?"

divine knowledge is Your most majestic blessing
the moment You open the door of the universe
no one realises
You wish to introduce Yourself
yet all the presentations of deeds
are mere tokens
reciprocated with tokens
the seed of love
which is not buried
in the earth
will not grow
as a perfect tree

the black sky is the heart
it only brightens
if God is seen in it
if you still cannot see Him
on the vast plain of this cosmos
you too will not see Him
in the everlasting hereafter
you need the bright light from the niche of the lamp
to see Him in yourself
there is nothing that veils Him
what is other than Him is still Him
like the glistening glass

untouched by fire
not in the east nor in the west
that glass is light, that light is glass
the refraction of His beauty
evident in everything

truly God is not hidden
so to reach Him
is it necessary to find proof
truly God is not far either
from the carpet of this cosmos
so to unite the self with Him
is there a need for a veil to separate
the eye of your heart itself witnesses
your being is non-existent
do not ride the mule
from a realm to another realm
you have to migrate and leave immediately
all the realms of His creation
and reflect
where does He place you now
by Your love I beg
do not banish this self from You
when I arrive in front of Your door
do not distant this self from You
when I approach Your boundary

passion has prompted me to appear before You
after imprisoning me as a captive
You are my saviour
at the battlefield of love

now how can I speak in private with You
as soon as the battle is over
the whole cosmic plain vanishes
within Your throne

I thirst for a drink
from the glass of Your Love so pristine
how can I express
You truly exist
within this heart coated with earthly dust
You often walk on the Sahara desert of my heart
bringing my soul with You
for the sake of the passionate love for You
I am expelled from the laymen's glorification of God
poetry makes our communication more loving and
intimate
from the spoken invocation on the lips
all desires in the heart vanished
as soon as I see You approach
bringing genuine hopes
without feeling the love of Your blessings
I will not know myself
I am truly certain
to have witnessed You in my heart
yet the one who sees You outwardly
thinks this earth is not a place of Your visit
You exist forever
on the throne of Your sky
the night after prayer
they return home and close the doors of Your house
they turn off all the lights
they vacate Your niche till dawn
while the hearts of those who never sleep
throughout the night

can see You so clear and evident
they seek forgiveness from You
before the arrival of the promised death

Arriving At The Throne Of Love

this teaching is like a long flowing river
not requiring a voyage guide, just prepare a vessel
travel as far as possible

sojourn at the lake of the heart, will unveil the other lakes
in the fresh water with the fragrance of roses and pine
beautiful birds twittering in flight
but follow the flute's melody by the piper who is unseen
the song of praise continues to invite you
to the gardens of colorful roses

do not stop at the base of despair
if your vessel has not reached its destination
rays of hope still await
with the celebration of glorious light

hurry come down to the river
even if the person who loves you dearly
threatens you with the swift currents
do not let yourself feel small and hindered
life is just like pet fishes
in a trapped glass aquarium that smells bad
accompanied by lumps of pebbles
you ought to be a dignitary

owning acres of farmlands
as long as your eyelids become a hindrance
thus unable to see the whole realm of truth
go to all the bazaars in the world
ask the merchants in the apparel shops
are there garbs that are more expensive
than the garb of existence which is not coloured by
personal egoism

do you not realise what you are looking for
when you visit the site of the green plantation
surely a sweetness that is hidden

is in the secret of the ripened fruits
if that is truly your destination
you are indeed looking for who you are
your body resembles an upright sugarcane plant
hard and arrogant
squeeze it till finely crushed
till the sweet soul drips
that is genuine sugar
be like the bees, savour the sweetness
to the heart's content
while swimming in the ocean of honey
neither does it drown nor its wings break
now exit from time and enter the bazaar
you have to be willing to support yourself
without expecting assistance from others
just sell all your material wealth
which is no longer needed in your life
so your journey will not be burdened

and its profits you invest into the eternal life
but do not sell your patched torn robe
with the lowest price
in the future you will be mocked
by those too ignorant to understand
the essence of life which you have treaded upon

the world is vicinity of a prison
its sun lies beneath the dark solid ground
its wonders will not bring benefit
if you are not diligent in getting it
enrich the green landscape of the farms and plantations
sprouting fruits and fragrant flowers
celebrate this happy day
like giving a banquet during a wedding ceremony
all the guests are our friends
this is not a mere illusion
the truth is we have arrived at the point of evolution
one day you will sit pondering
cursing all nightmares

which tarnished the mirror of your heart
caused by complacency in the heated cauldron of thought
whilst in the vast spiritual garden
its fruits offered a dose of taste
more delicate, cooler and calmer
accepting the wonders
without weighing intellect and proof

love emits a vapour
from earth and water
spreading the wings of the birds of paradise
only when you exhale your breath
from the nest of a sincere heart

divine knowledge is like Abraham
who felt the experience of fire in its true sense
not arguing about smoke or global warming
hieroglyphs of the Sufi
not written on empty papers
except chiselled on the mountain of the heart as white as
snow
do not write poetry to hunt for a pen name
be His genuine poet
be quiet, let Him alone directly speak
through your poems
your tongue is a palace gate
you too know who lives in it
shut that gate as tightly as possible
for the sake of the wealth
which has to be constantly guarded
and that wealth has never been left by its owner
the heart is not merely a glass wall
which disperses Allah's Light
yet that is the main gate
which paves directly to the unseen realms
get used to seeing the light around
not only from the rear window of your silent room
look with light upon light
lest the window frame finally breaks

so your eyes will not be dazzled by the sight

the true mosque is the realisation of your soul
this is the prayer hall for worshippers
without being calculative of time
they delve into the blessings of Allah
at a level where the whole universe has not been created
they recognize existence
before the physical being was born
they see seeds
before the cultivation produces paddy and wheat
they search for jewels
even though there are no vast oceans

the sky and the earth
too narrow to contain His presence
He only resides on a vast throne
that is filled with love in the hearts of His lovers
find Him there
He wishes you to know Him
at a meeting so intimate
the moment He shares secrets with you
love has accompanied you to the niche of that love itself
love offers sweetness to all bitterness
love moulds lead into gold
love enriches the green paddy after it withers
love proposes to the king to be a commoner

don't you reckon
it is too easy to acquire divine knowledge
that you have known who yourself is
release that image of yourself
as long as you only gaze upon your own image
which is within the frame of the theatrical mirror
you will not get to see Him
you are not you
you are a vast ocean
in it there are millions of you
diving

said the worshipper, He is in front
whereas by His truth
the worshipper is non-existent
like a cloth that is dyed
once submerged
the entire cloth changes with no colour
the worshipper is what He envisions
like painting a rose in a rose garden
that is how He expresses love
not as a cage of slavery
all doors open
from the rose petals
He is the One who narrates the verses of His roses
He is the One who finds His Own Love
He is the One Who falls in love with His Own beauty

Love At Mount Palmer

between Mount Palmer[24] and Mount Judi[25],
there is a sky dome
and like Columbus entering the dock door of love,
slowly my ship anchored in the ocean
which is no longer turbulent with violent waves
to the shores of the lagoon, now appears
the desert horizon

a golden carpet develops stock warehouses
skyscrapers, universal competition that is hectic and
frenzied crossing traffic hunting for the champion
gamecock separated from treading the roots of the
historical village.
The abode of life even though free but still feels
imprisoned by the potholes of anxiety, like isolated
from the many species of fish inhabitants which
are forced to share the alleys of the glass aquarium,
drowning torturing corals life shrouded by the material
wind which hardens the image of the city's dreams.

Noah, like your ark stranded high on the peak
of Mount Judi, now I am a friend of the vowed dove,
coming from a distant land yearning for the
compassionate light of the heart
on a handful of earth at the foot of that ancient hill which
nearly became extinct being violated by excavators of
development and isolated silently from the screams of
this mirage-city.
I grasp for the highest stairs to visit
the raised shrine of the ascetic lover. At the sojourned
peak of Mount Palmer I meet with the timeless charming
echoes

[24] it is located in the one of the world's busiest port zone in the middle of cosmopolitan Singapore. At the peak of Mount Palmer, there is a tomb of a saint of Allah named Saiyid Noh Bin Muhammad Al Habsyi, commonly known as Habib Noh.
[25] mountain that is mentioned in the Quran Surah Hud : 44. At its peak lies the ark of Noah.

from the niche of the melodious verses of prayer,
conveying my perceived devoted supplication
to the birds of Attar, come for a moment
winged assembly at the solitary corridor
of the beloved's shrine
and celebrate this joyous day of Asyura[26]. Noah,
are there now true friends like
your friends who are still loyal to their pledge
of allegiance to the covenant, descended from your ark of
brotherhood
to the ruins of the barren land
to unite again the valley of hope
after the world was devastated by the flood of Tsunami?

the green dome parts the cosmic expanse
for centuries this hidden rose garden hill
becomes a treasured monument which preserves
the secret of the sky, I rip this door of soul-searching,
I dive into peaceful discernment so miraculous
like being at the beautiful peak of Thursina
which conveys Moses's yearning at the moment
approaching the veiled light of Your Image,
when will the mirror-heart of The One be revealed,
for what purpose is this aged world disguised by
the masks of cosmetic revolution
if the true beauty of The Lover's Image
is not seen throughout the universal garden?
greetings Habib Noh[27], peace be upon you o saint,
at the highest door of your shrine radiates the fragrance
of natural musk, smoothing the smitten wings of
the poet's dove which still roam
searching for the dimension of God's personality.
Yourself is the chief leader among the Sufi leaders
at the plains of the neglectful city which has lost its
caravan, you have eradicated the weeds of the heart
you have established the mosque of the roused love

---

[26] the tenth day in the month of Muharram in the Islamic calendar.
[27] Habib Noh – a saint of Allah named Saiyid Noh Bin Muhammad Al Habsyi
(1788 – 1866)

you have captured the peak of this self-mortification hill
like Noah who immediately housed his ark
after reading the signs of the height of the waves,
is it fitting for the hilly legacy of this Sufi
and all other historical hills
to be continuously guarded
from the traps of development
to become a protective fortress for this nation
in case the world is flooded again by the gigantic
Tsunami?

Haji Mohd Salleh Mosque, Mount Palmer
Singapore

Love Of The Night Of Power

tonight is the Night of Power

let us all unite in the night of a thousand months
we leave behind
arguments with shadows

truly, tonight is the Night of Power
we will see Him
like we are looking at the full moon floating
in the eternal paradise

that month is the most glorious among a thousand
months
view a thousand in one view
one in a thousand
in a thousand we are of one mother

moon, descend upon the palms of our hands
offer your light
to the earth that is increasingly suffering
pitch dark

As Zulaikha[28]

no need for you to glance from afar
come here and pick the blossoms
in this forbidden olive garden
teach me the meaning of His everlasting love
even if your sleeves will be torn
by the touch of the abrasive thorns from this wounded
garden
come o Joseph
there is no beauty except the beauty of your face
evident across the shoulder of the whole universe

you appear all of a sudden
when I was also still searching for a way out
from every secret corridor in this palace
as soon as I caught sight of the radiance of your face
the cloudy sky seemed to open
all the seven domains of its doors
like the sparkling sword refracting the coalition
of a rainbow

release me from the heart of this palace
which has for decades tortured my soul
fettered by the existence of a king
my lonely soul truly longs to touch you, Joseph
are you the glorious love

which descends from the peak of the sky
bedewing the path of the journey's warm meadows
never have I felt before
such a mysterious presence like this
in the crannies of the barren valley of my life
I know it is not easy for me to escape
fleeing from the huge and many-layered doors
of the palace

---

[28] Zulaikha was the wife of the chief minister in ancient Egypt who could not resist the handsome Prophet Yusuf or Joseph, and her obsession with him caused her sleepless nights.

while the birds are flying at the break of dawn
pecking their invocations from tree to tree
in the eyes of my wings, emerges the gem of your face
as an eternal soul
I wish to instantly approach your sacred place
praying in silence before God whom you worship
I can no longer conceal the shadows of my humiliation
after being ridiculed by all the maidens of the palace
am I insane to yearn for the light of your love
so that you are enticed to feel
my silken yearning which has no boundary

when a vessel set sail alone
amidst the turbulent waves
in my palanquin of delirium,
I call out your name repeatedly
Joseph, do not go far from me!
I do not have any friends
in this confusing journey
how shall I differentiate

between truth and falsehood
between the glow of love and lustful temptations
this mystifying lesson I cannot understand
from books on interpretation
yet I am sure beneath the fluttering eye of my heart
so serene
there is a realm of truth where God resides
and you are a gem most precious
who is brilliant in hiding the equator
amidst the ocean of passion

love for you makes all the stars
shine in the sky, the moon and the sun
fall in prostration on the prayer mat of your dreams
love for you charms
all the beautiful maidens in the palace
like fishes jumping out of the clear river
because they are infatuated with your charming looks

Joseph, bring me with you
everywhere even to the invisible continent
I am not hesitant to abandon
all treasures of the kingdom
I will remove all the bejewelled bracelets from my hand
because today I truly understand
true love is a delicate shawl of divinity
the secrets of God can only be known from within
is this called Arafah[29]

which enjoins the will of God
"I am the hidden treasure
I want Myself to be known..."
Joseph, I am that sinful lady most disgraceful
audaciously flouting the etiquette by opening the door of
your chamber
nearly am I separated from the embrace of my shawl
like a leaf fallen and floundering from a tree
unsteadily tossed by the swift waves
and tempest
I am willing to sacrifice my whole body
yet in the end I too am a lady most forlorn
failing to seduce you as a genuine ark
without me realizing, I have grabbed the robe
of your love
and I was audacious enough to veil a slander
for sheer fear and shame to be censured with punishment
and contempt

truly Joseph, your prison you much preferred
than the amorous persuasion of a lady
even though enthroned in a palatial glittering palace
since I have opened your door
give me a little chance and forgiveness
to find a resting place on the threshold

---

[29] Arafah is the name of the desert located on the eastern part of Mecca. It is an important place in Islam because during the Hajj, pilgrims spend the afternoon there on the ninth day of Zulhijjah, supplicating to Allah to forgive their sins and praying for personal strength in the future.

of mortal misery
I am certain eleven stars, sun and moon
that prostrated at the domain of your sky
are all now present
in the deepest niche of the secret of my heart

Wedding

during the wedding shrieking laughter was heard
from the voices of the ladies in the kitchen
unceasingly they glorify
how charming is the groom named Yusuf
till unknowingly the knife in hand
finally cut their own hands
blood then drips
on a tray of food

this wedding is an impressive fiesta
its occasion will always be remembered
in slumber for days
we joke, play and sometimes grief
by bittersweet myths
yet despite the truth
we are serious in facing it

this wedding removes veil after veil
for a moment we are together in the sleeping chamber
we discover what is truly more precious
unlikely for us to exchange
with all the others
the entire silence in the sleeping chamber
mixed with the fragrance of the soul

Sky Garden

You too pulled Joseph out
from the well unknown to passers-by
You too reserved a place for Jonah
in a secret chamber in the belly of the whale
so how is it possible this journey in search of You
can proceed with these very feet
by only wearing Your white sandals
Jacob found again his Joseph who was lost
sitting smiling on a throne

from the distant morn lingered a fragrance
of grilled glutinous rice
Fansuri[30] is very hungry yearning for You
at the final pillar
this mystical truth how shall I explain
he finds Your Image in his own abode
now the tragic drops of his blood squirted onto my neck
I yearn for a companion who understands
the souls which send vessels to the trail of Your garden
without Your manifestation, impossible for me to arrive
at Your door

the dews on my grass do not wish to dry up
even if Your dawn has risen
thus lifting the blanket which draped my slumber
yet I do not want to budge
from the embrace of Your existence
I still reminisce that midnight prayer of love
even if You gleam a moment's
sheen of Your gaze upon me
I am sure You appear to fulfill all my wishes
so I surrender all that is Yours
that is attached on my body
if that is the condition You seek for the meeting
so that I do not only keep my own life

---

[30] a Malay sufi poet Hamzah Fansuri

in the chest of eternity
now I can see You smiling from the grieving clouds
I do not wish to lose You
true love has no binding constraints
how I yearn to join
the birds of Attar
flying to the mountains, descending to the inner valleys
rivers of nerves flowing rapidly before me
the universe is the origin of all scriptures of Yours
that is widely spread
offering millions of knowledge that You Exist
so what is the shortest way
to reach You
with the fatigued birds
throughout the journey
I sojourn to Your paddy fields, Love
myself appears as a grain of paddy that twirls
in the swirling wind that has no end
in every grain of paddy
surely there is a trail that leads to Your Existence

in Your sky garden, You make me eternal
birds of Attar merrily flying
building nests in my heart
I know my love will blossom here, in spring
to wherever the intuitive eyes gaze upon
there hang the orchid blooms
beneath the lush lote tree,
I grow anxious waiting for You
my heartbeat searching for the trodden path
when will You arrive
from dawn till dusk, I only fill the ballad
of my invocation
because I know not what other tasks
I have to do except this
I have no knowledge of You
no idea in what way I shall greet Your arrival
how elated will I be, if You come
only to hear my ballad

I will always serve new poems
all images of dreams preserved in the hut of my soul
no longer will I be able to hide them any more
I hope You will soon come
because days on this earth that are covered with dust and
mud
will quickly pass like wind, lonesome and ephemeral
I wish for You to be by my side, singing

in this sky garden
the closer I am to You,
I see the earth becoming darker and lusterless
bring me to fly far with the birds of Attar
Your entire universe I will explore

in Your sky garden, I whisper to the stars
why were you instructed to prostrate to Joseph?
to the beauty of Joseph's image,
there is a veil that cannot be lifted
"One more step," said Gabriel, "my entire existence will
perish!"
Love,
it is not You who is said to be distant from the
imagination of Your poet
I am the one who is distant, because I do not see Your
Face personally
Your Face does not need an oil lamp that is brightly lit
Your Face is the witness of Your truth
there is no beauty like Your Face
there is no imperfection which denies Your perfection
this world is a fragment
of the spark of light of Your glory
a moment away from You, only for the sake of an
understanding
You are no longer different from Yourself
even though there are voices instigating
me to leave Your sky garden,

stop this poetry

yet I will not remove the King's robe
You have given me freedom
with this robe of existence
my poems have no desire for an audience
the eulogy of my hopes perch not on the wings
of a horse
flying to reach the sun
because what is purer and clearer
is to see the river of Your love
which flows downwards from the fissures of the
mountainous heart
and to the birds of Attar
I give full sincerity in my song

each soul wishes a different rice dish
yet in the self, there is an eternal dish
enter this sky garden
do not fret about the similarity in the skin of fruits
His cultivated fruits have never rot
even if Joseph appears ugly
in the hateful eyes of his brothers
yet Joseph is the most charming
in the intuitive eyes of Jacob
till when do you want to associate God
with His creations
all proofs apart from Him, no longer
have any significance
no matter how thick the cloudy sky
that you gaze upon a dew drop
still originates from the vast ocean
you are His Existence too

in Your sky garden, You still wait for a reply
from the love letters which You sent
to the deafness of the world
You prefer the small oil lamps
in each home of Your lovers
to the stars scattered
across the galaxy

ah, where have You hidden
the tranquility of Your love
when the singing of Your night
does not fill the air in the bazaars of the world
before the break of Your dawn, I hear
the sun saying,
"Each time there is a replacement for my duty,
I am ashamed of my emptiness!"

come to this sky garden, spring will change
there is light from the waxing moon, grapes
which will not intoxicate
hearts of lovers, growing amidst
blossoms of olives
if you wish to visit, there is no problem
even if you do not wish to visit,
there is also no problem

Gardening in Rumi's Land

I have entered Your garden, invite me to speak
Your mesmerizing beauty makes me more reserved
even though this not the rainy season
and my footsteps did not even get stuck
on the wet grass
You have brighten up this eternal day
birds chatter with one another
at the master's arena of love
I do not know what I have to learn
from the signs of the blooming flowers
a companion like myself can only share
a piece of tasteless bread
on the face of a small plate
which is too shy to gaze upward towards the sky

fruits in Your garden urge me
"bring the plate closer, look at the Face
without a veil
do not be embarrassed about your gift
the tasteless bread is a gift from My inspired one
who owns nothing except true love
now come and feast at the King's banquet
feel My Existence and remain everlasting in My will
you will discover what you have been looking for
it is truly yourself at the end of the journey
the goal of life is to witness Me
on the prayer mat of your reality"

in the land of Rumi, I do not know how to dance
the swift dance that whirls
following the swaying movement of the sword
the drum of my heart has absolutely no sound
to its melody
how can I then penetrate the network of the sky
teach me a different way, the secret of submission
far closer to Your Existence
so that I can quickly reveal in the cup

"only God"
squeezing clear juice
from the fibrous sugarcane stem
its residue dissolved in the earth
its sweetness enjoyed by the sky
into God's hiding place

gardening in Rumi's land
repeatedly I lived and died as a seed
in the lumps of earth with aflamed longing
before the image of Your whirling sky
and emerges a garden
from the garden You divided
all these hidden treasures
to reveal Yourself
in the reflection of the universe
You serve drinks
without grapes that are intoxicating
You grant satiation
without differentiating rice, meat and vegetables
You present an apparel for the King
without the golden throne of luxury
You chain the pearls of rain
without shrouding the grieving clouds
You teach wisdom
without a teacher and writing
You ignite the sun
without hurting the earth and the moon
You manifest the garden of Your Existence
without expelling the birds

Bread From The Sky

the bread from the sky which you serve can fill
this age. This is my small plate from the drought of dust.
This is my hunger which cannot be sold in the bazaar of
poetry. The hunger which has long become the secret of a
poem perplexing the intellect. When will that absolute
day of happiness arrive, the day that separates the birds
from the cage door of this world.

the aroma of your bread entices the birds of the heart
to fly freeing all self-attachments, returning to digest
the meal of your love and bread quickly absorbed to
the core of the heart becoming the contemplation of a
strong valley and the throne dais for the true Emperor, at
the primordial realm where the heart was created before
other creations exist.

your bread is unlike the grapes of the earth which
intoxicate. Yet your bread can motivate a grieving friend
to be happy, offer a relaxing bed in an affectionate
atmosphere without enemies, will change an evil
personality to one who is immaculate in character and
speech, expedite new breath for this universe.
today offer your bread as much as possible to those
who are suffering in the continent
of hunger.

The Price Of A Mistake

sorry, last night I entered your kitchen without your
permission. You were fast asleep alone in your room
while hugging tightly the picture of your child and wife. I
opened the cabinet drawer and pulled out
a knife. I wanted to cut meat or fish. I rummaged through
the refrigerator but I could not find any meat or fish,
there was only a serving of your daughter's birthday cake
on which you will light up the candles the following day.

sorry, I cut first a slice from your daughter's birthday
cake, before you could even light up those candles, even
before you could hear the returning stamping sound of
your wife's and daughter's shoes at the doorway. Outside
the weather is dark and drizzling, there are still cats
corresponding, dogs howling, they have yet to discover
the hut of the world which is peaceful and lasting. From
the neighbor's house, vaguely audible the latest news
from the radio:
countless bombs exploded at Karbala. Sacred buildings
became the enraged target of a fiery war. Yet chemical
weapons which became the search mission have yet to be
found beneath the layers of the land of Iraq. At the base of
the Indian Ocean an earthquake occurred. The entire
Banda Aceh was destroyed in the blink of an eye drowned
by the gigantic wave called Tsunami, dead bodies were
strewn beneath the heap exactly like rotten fish dumped
off at the wholesale market. Only an ancient mosque was
left standing firmly through the centuries.

sorry, I have no right to enter your kitchen. But before
you awake from your slumber, I have returned the knife
to its original storage place,
I have lighted up those candles on your daughter's
birthday cake.

This Home Which You Sojourn

this home which You sojourn
does not need a myriad of lights
which are very bright
to show proof as to where You reside
the presence of Your Image itself is proof
which needs no proof
on the day when people come in throngs
to the forum table
laying out various assignments
debates and objections

Debater Of Death

he was prepared waiting for the arrival of the angel of
death instead the accursed devil came, challenging him to
a debate.

argument after argument of the devil was defeated so
easily. Finally the devil admitted that he was not an
ordinary man to debate within the religious field.

"But if you can answer my final question, I promise
not to hound you in the final moments of your death."

"Ask then. Truly you have been given many
opportunities to harass people.

"How is your faith in God?" asked the devil.

he was speechless for a moment. He tried to think of an
answer but there was no answer. This time he thought he
would be defeated in the hands of the devil.

"I do not have any proof of how I have faith in God!" he
surrendered.

"You are right!" answered the devil and left.

In The Ascetic's Chamber

the electric lights in the ascetic's chamber suddenly went
off. He came out looking for Comel[31] which wandered off
to an unknown place that night. Outside the weather was
so bad peltered with heavy rain,
non-stop since dawn. Lightning and thunder were
mutually corresponding in the sky. Meander upon
meander fast flowing and its murky water increasingly
flooding the surface of the land. He felt helpless to
continue searching for Comel in the middle of that storm
and fog, his beloved
Persian cat.

he believed Comel was not lost and was just hiding
in a funnel somewhere. All these years as an ascetic, he
was happy with Comel that liked to sit meditating
quietly, as if Comel too did not bother about life of this
mortal world.

upon returning and sitting in his ascetic chamber which
was still pitch-dark,
suddenly he touched something next to his prayer mat.
He groped,
"Oh you're here apparently."
He stroked and caressed the head of that adorable

little one with thick fur. The little one did not move
shrinking
its body but its voice continues to be silent without
mewing like always.

approaching dawn, suddenly the electric lights in that
ascetic's chamber brightened up again. He woke up from
his sleep. What a startle and his eyes were fixed on – by
his side   apparently was not Comel as he thought, but

---

[31] Comel is the name for the Persian cat

a little puppy with thick fur similar to Comel.

"If the condition last night in this chamber was not pitch dark, certainly my body will not be caressed by the hands of this pious and holy man," said the little puppy as it left the ascetic's chamber.

After Self-Reflection
And Revelation Of The Sky

the one that was secretly asked for was a frangipani
the fallen one was a dried lizard

The Serpent's Apparel

finally, it turns out to be a serpent
who else in the shade of that vegetation
can change layer upon layer
the color of its apparel
never does it feel embarrassed
each time it appears naked before the mirror
with its beautiful body coiling
but its tongue full of venomous gossips
perpetually cursing the sky
ever since it slips and falls into
the deep well, suddenly it realizes
in that bottomless depth
it fails to climb again
the stairways to the garden of paradise

if only from the start it knows
how tormenting the curse is
perhaps it will not be bold to perch
on the rim of that forbidden well
passionately its ruby eyes spied
from the gaps in the undergrowth of that dark vegetation
in a garden without chatting souls
enquiring the rustling secrets of the kingdom of water
quietly it hears
a loud song of illusion
vibrating in the niche of the truth of the universe

strange, behind the apparel of this mortal realm
there are apparels for other realms
like a lake preserving the sun
till it unexpectedly discovers
at the bottom of the heart of that deep well
lies buried a chest of humanitarian dignity
as soon as it is opened
it found remnants of a country's map
that is almost destroyed
following the final lineage

one day it was chased around the entire city
by people wielding choppers in their hands
they chopped off its head
chopped off its tail
hacked its body into pieces
its blood blended with the earth
the cause of the mistake it says,

"humans are just like me
will slither far on the surface of the earth
each time the apparel of the serpent changes
for the sake of searching for the lineage"

The Pilgrimage Of A Sufi

when he was about to depart for Baitullah[32]
you wished to join his journey
for a moment he thought, were you able
to be patient with him
his entourage did not carry a large amount
of the earth's wealth
his entourage was not a part of a group of tourists
his entourage consisted of Allah's guests
who only submitted to Allah
invocating and supplicating
reminiscing the call of the pilgrimage

when he observed you struggling
with a huge luggage full of excess attire
immediately he extended both his hands
shouldering the load which burdened you
although there was no need for you to bring it
into the aircraft cabin
so that your body could sit and rest comfortably
and your heart could remain serene envisaging Allah
without worrying about life's problems
which you had left behind

when the entourage arrived at the City of Medina
the scorching midday light burst out

from behind the mountains
he noticed that you were so tired and weary
after travelling across the wide and distant desert
instantly he ran to the bazaar
thinking you would be extremely hungry
when he returned and knocked on your hotel room door
he offered you a kebab pita
which was freshly grilled
when he saw you walking with a limp

---

[32] or the Kaabah, which is located in Mecca, one of the holy cities in Islam.

leaving your hotel room for the Prophet's Mosque
at each call of prayer
he noticed traces of blood and cuts
on the sole of your feet
instantly he rushed to the pharmacy
searching for an antidote
so your feet would heal quickly
and you would not continue
to bear the pain and grumble
when dealing with the trials and tribulations from Allah
while retreating in the Prophet's Mosque
he noticed that you often sat far away from Raudah[33]
and only once you visited the Prophet's Tomb,
Abu Bakar's[34] Tomb and Umar's[35] Tomb
ever since you arrived at the City of Medina
how good if you could use the opportunity
that was so short that day
so that you could learn truly
the meaning of love and struggle
before you moved to Mecca

between Mecca and Medina
each night he never slept
on a soft mattress in the hotel room
because there were many family members
occupying the limited space in the room
the moment he laid his body
shivering on the red carpet
withstanding the cold
at the lower edge of the bed, his eyes glanced wistfully
at his wife's face and his adorable children's faces
sleeping soundly shimmered by dim hazy lights
momentarily he remembered you perhaps having a cozy
honeymoon in the adjacent room
by right you should share the room with his children
or paid the incremental fee

---

[33] Raudah is a sacred place in the Prophet's Mosque.
[34] Prophet Muhammad beloved companions
[35] Prophet Muhammad beloved companions

for being placed in a room for two
but he was willing to sacrifice
for the sake of your happiness
because he often witnessed the two of you
husband and wife
senior citizens
mutually hostile and lack of understanding
throughout a shared marriage.

thus which of the grace of God that you denied
till up comes hatred and malice
you ostracized him
from those who were not chosen by you
disliked watching him getting too close
to The Closest One
at the end of each circumambulation
at the edge of Baitullah
he often got to kiss the Black Stone

"o Lover The Closest One
I wish to be as close to You as possible
even if love for You
will make Your creatures jealous of me
You have granted me the ability of the eye of the heart
to perceive inwardly
if You want the eye of my heart to be strong
and sensitive towards You
avert me even the size of an atom from this world
anything that obscures my longing Sahara."

on the way back to homeland
he helped you a lot
carrying the things which you bought
from the Holy Land
he sympathized when he saw you walking with a limp
because your feet sustained injury
as a result of the arrogant words which you uttered
in front of the Kaabah
thus which of the grace of God that you denied

till you turned away your face from looking at him
when he visited your home on the morning
of one feast day
in a white robe which he bought on his pilgrimage

As A Spider
At The Entrance Of Thur Cave

when we are tracking the path to this cave
there are still many slabs of stone and gravel
around the housing estate
yet it does not hinder the journey

we eventually reach the door of the sky
the rain of mercy is still drizzling
approaching dusk
soaking the earthy porch of An-Nur Mosque

Is it You who opened the door of the sky
bestowing the light to the atmosphere
the night is most beautiful
lulled by the calming poetry of Al-Amin
resonating through the white porch of An-Nur Mosque

span your view across the clear starlit sky
span your view across the valleys of the mountains
span your view across the sandy desert with no boundary
span your view across the green shady date palms
span your view across the glorious Shining City
there is where a holy Prophet
who loves his people very much
invocate and express your salutations

sincerely to him
upon the enduring spider web
we used as a prayer mat
tonight we are the martyred spiders
armored with poetry
before the door of Thur Cave
even if we are defeated by the enemies' swords
we will still defend
the light of this cave
because in it

there is Al-Amin[36] and Abu Bakar

---

[36] Prophet Muhammad

There Is Love At The Valley
Of The Foot Of That Mountain

at the valley of the foot of that mountain suddenly Moses
hears

"Oh God, where are You now?
Your Image I have never seen
If I become a slave serving You
I will shine Your shoes
so there will not be a speck of dust
at all stuck onto Your shoes
I will comb Your hair
when You want to groom before the mirror
I will wash Your robe
so Your robe will always appear pristine and shiny
I will bring a serving of milk for You
for meals in the morning and night
I will kiss Your hands and feet
for my obedience and loyalty to You
I will prepare Your bed
when Your eyes begin to feel sleepy
I will look after Your house
so Your house will always look spick-and-span
oh God, who am I
only a male shepherd
me and the sheep are all Yours truly."

Moses who has been listening with a sense of wonder
then shouted

"O shepherd!
watch your words and repent
God is not like what you think!"

suddenly a divine voice intervened

"O Moses, don't you separate him from Me
are you sent to unite
or separate?
I have bestowed upon each of My servants
his own way of praising Me
both from the viewpoint, language
and soulful expression towards Me
but it is not easy for you to understand
each variation in their praises
that looks wrong to you, but correct to him
poison is a killer to one person
perhaps a cure for others
whether in holiness or disgrace
whether those who are diligent or lazy to worship Me
how much exalted My name is praised by My devotees
all that is not a benchmark for Me
what I gaze upon and value is the humility
in My servants
no matter where you direct your prayer mat
you are still facing My Image."

Moses finally realizes
what is borne out of the language of that shepherd
is the light from the spirit
realm there is no restriction or rule
in praising God
that is true devotion
attributes of God and attributes of man unite
if not for the greatness of His Love
the entire universe will be silent
without any language

The Throne Of Water

that small butterfly knows, far in that forest interior there is an isolated well. It once flew there, at one point it was lost because it was abandoned by its friends. It hears a voice calling it from a distance, but it does not care because it is not satisfied yet with playing in a garden, it is engrossed frolicking with the fragrant blossoms, joyful and laughing. When the traces of dusk are vanishing, then it realizes it is separated far from its friends. It is confused and does not know where else to track its friends. It flies just anywhere following trails that are arduous with twists and turns.

as it can no longer fly in the darkness of the atmospheric space, it then stops not knowing where it is. Soon dawn breaks, suddenly it is surprised feeling like it is present at the site of a throne, surrounded by slabs of gigantic boulders, covered by lush foliage like a door which has never been opened to the outside world. It hears the splashing sound of water and apparently there is a well whose water is most calm and clear.
maybe there is never a human traveller who sojourns here apart from birds and other insects, he thinks. It then feels excited wishing to play on the
waters of that well, it settles at the side of a rock whilst sipping a few drops of water which feels so cold and believes that the well water will never dry up forever. After quenching its thirst, it then flies to tease the blossoms around the site of that throne never has it seen such blossoms in other gardens, so beautiful and truly captivating.

a few days later, it comes again to that well but this time it brings its friends. It is shocked to see the well water has dried up. Indeed it cannot believe and wonders where has the well water relocated? It feels disappointed when accused of lying by its friends thus forsaking it alone floundering at the site of that throne.

it flies back and forth to find proof of how the well water
has dried up. Suddenly it spots a hut standing not far from
there. It then flies quickly
in the direction of that hut and through the open window
it sneaks in. It sees a young man holding a pen between
his right hand fingers and it
witnesses from the tip of that pen flows a fluid that
engraves verse after verse on the page of a book. In that
hut there was a cabinet filled with hundreds of books.

"Surely this young man is the one who uses up all
the well water," said that small butterfly. It now believes
that the well dries up because it is used as

ink by that young man, resulting in the production of
hundreds of books. It too does not want to miss the
opportunity and thus descends upon the tip of that young
man's pen while gulping to its heart's content the
wellspring which flows forth.

that young man is moved and feels great sympathy
watching that thirsty little butterfly, like a weary
wayfarer searching for water in a desert. He does not
disturb it and leaves alone to drink as much ink that is
desired by that little creature.

that night, that young man suddenly dreams being
present in God's throne.

"Do you know, how you are able to be in My Presence?"

"For my good deeds in writing so as to spread knowledge
to mankind."

"No! You apparently are approaching My Hell because
you feel conceited about your writings!"

"If that is so, please explain to me O Lord! What

truly saves me from the brink
of Your Hell and helps me to arrive here in Your
Presence?"

"Due to the sincerity in your heart to give water to a
thirsty butterfly
in its journey searching for water!"

A Conversation In The Garden Of Paradise

there is a ram talking to its friends
on a widely spread grassy meadow. "Praise to the Lord
who has placed us in this garden of paradise. Each day we
do not run out of grasses to graze here. Each blade of
grass that we chew, will regenerate new grasses."

"But strangely, all along when we eat the grass, why are
our bodies not thin like the grass? We are not what we
swallowed. If only we can become the grass, surely there
is not one among us who will ask anxiously, "Who is
willing to be the sacrifice this time, brother?" said another
ram.

Reason For Refusing To Enter Paradise

before closing the Quran recitation class that night,
as usual the religious teacher would tell a story to his
young pupils. This time the religious teacher wishes to
relate about paradise which has been promised by God
for the faithful believers as mentioned in the holy Quran.

the religious teacher continues, "Paradise is exceptionally
beautiful and cannot be compared to any other things on
this earth. Its surrounding is full of greenery. In paradise
there are gardens widely spread, there are trees and
fruits of various kinds and in pairs just like the banana
trees, dates and pomegranates. Fruits can be picked from
a close range. There are a few types of rivers which flow
like the milk river, the honey river and the wine river.
There is a lake and a wellspring which gushes out. There
are palaces in it await chaste maidens with sparkling
eyes, good manners and exquisite looks. So beautiful are
these chaste maidens that they are like rubies, pearls and
corals. Their skin is delicate, glowing white, never
touched by man or jinn. They relax on soft green
cushions, couches enthroned with gold and jewels as well
as exotic carpets with interiors made of silk thread. They
bring cups and glasses filled with beverages from
flowing water. Those beverages are not intoxicating. They
offer fruits based on the desired choices of the dwellers
while serving with respect and affection. Paradise is a
place that is permanent and everlasting."

the pupils were awed listening to the story by the
religious teacher. After ending the story, the religious
teacher wants to test his pupils.

"Those who want to accompany me to paradise, please
raise your hands!"
apparently many pupils instantaneously raise
their hands, on their faces are signs of excitement
and happiness. Certainly not a single one wants to be left

out from accompanying the religious teacher to paradise.
Yet there is one pupil who does not want to raise his hand
and his expression looks so silent and dejected.
the religious teacher then asks that reserved pupil,

"Why do you refuse to raise your hand?"

"I do not want to follow you to paradise! Because just now
my father reminded me. Right after reciting the Quran do
not go anywhere else. Go home straight away!"

this time the religious teacher was dumbfounded.

Mystic Love

the illuminated heart affirms the yearning to glance at the
soul of the field day I am the one arousing a voice from
silence which never have I uttered during the moments
when I will return to the soul of Your Longing
and my coming back here is just to take off this robe, truly
I have seen You with the entire eye of my soul

the bamboo leaves are now stunted beneath the rays of
sun at the time when I was floundering pulling that
dagger which stabbed my chest, unexpectedly my life will
be buried in this chamber of love and my blood returns as
semen that unites with Your secret

my semen is like dew
which falls on the rose
petals

About the Author

His true name according to family history is Raden Johar bin Raden Abdul Majid (alias Buang) bin Raden Muhammad Agus bin Raden Muhammad Ali Nuh bin Raden Agung (alias Nung Chik) bin Raden Abdur Rahman. His family tree has its roots in Palembang. The writer is also well known by his pseudonym H.B. Johar, apart from the common use of his name Johar Buang.

His paternal grandmother came from the Hadramaut, Yemen. His paternal great grandparents, Syekh Ibrahim Ar-Raqi and Ummu Zafran, travelled from Hadramaut to Singapore on a trading business. Whereas his maternal grandfather migrated from Palembang to Singapore, who was said to have run away from a mansion of an aristocratic family because of a family feud involving wealth and prestige. He then followed a trading ship which sailed the entire Malay archipelago. While residing in Singapore, his maternal grandfather married an Arab lady, Saiyidah Fatimah binte Syekh Johar.

His mother, Fatimah Binti Syekh Umar Bungsu, was of Bugis-Arab parentage and her family lineage can be traced to the Bugis royalty.

The writer was born in Singapore on 23 January 1958. His name, Johar, was given in honour of his paternal great grandfather Syekh Johar bin Syekh Ibrahim Ar-Raqi.

At the age of 13, he followed Thariqah Alawiyah. Then at the age of 16, he was under the tutelage of a Sufi master, Ustaz Syed Abdul Rahman Al-Kaff and later he was taught by another sufi master named Syekh Muhammad Thaha Al-Nur Muhammadi. Through the latter, he was granted the knowledge of the truth and knowing Allah. This knowledge was passed on by a great sufi master from India named Hazrat Khawaja Maulana Habibullah Syah Qutubul Ariffin Al-Qadariyyah Al-Chishtiyyah Al-Suhrawardiyyah Al-Sanusiyyah Al-Naqshabandiyyah Qudus Allah Sirah 'Aziz. Currently, the writer is more inclined towards the path and knowledge of the Sufi, Niche of Light Upon Light.

In his life journey as a writer, Johar has never enlisted in writing courses or received formal training from anyone. It was from the blessings of his teacher Syekh Muhammad Thaha Al-Nur Muhammadi that he began to develop an interest and received inspiration to write Sufi poems in the early 1980s.

His awards include the National Book Development Council of Singapore Book Award, National Art Council of Singapore Golden Point Award, Literature Prize Malay Language Council Singapore, Literature Award Darul Aman III Terengganu Malaysia, Islamic Poetry Prize Brunei Darussalam, Singapore Literature Prize 2010 and South East Asia Write Award 2010 in Thailand.

About The Editor And Translators

Fazidah Abu Bakar

Fazidah studied Geography, Political Science, English Language and Malay Language when she pursued her tertiary education at the National University of Singapore. She received her Diploma in Education from the National Institute of Education and taught Geography and English Language when she first started teaching more than two decades ago. Currently, she is the Art Coordinator in a secondary school

Nur Aisha Rahmat

Nur Aisha is a fulltime homemaker. She once worked as an English Language teacher in an Islamic school (Madrasah) in Singapore. She received a tertiary education from the National University of Singapore. Nur Aisha is the translator of a book entitled 'The Grand Saint Of Singapore' which recounted the life story of a holy man in Singapore named Habib Noh Bin Muhammad Al Habsyi.

Notes

www.ingramcontent.com/pod-product-compliance
Lightning Source LLC
Chambersburg PA
CBHW022028090426
42739CB00006BA/334